HOW TO READ
the
Universe

HOW TO READ THE UNIVERSE

Text by Susan McCann

An Hachette UK Company
www.hachette.co.uk

Summersdale Publishers Ltd
Part of Octopus Publishing Group Limited
Carmelite House
50 Victoria Embankment
LONDON
EC4Y 0DZ
UK

www.summersdale.com

Printed and bound in China

ISBN: 978-1-83799-191-4

Substantial discounts on bulk quantities of Summersdale books are available to corporations, professional associations and other organizations. For details contact general enquiries by telephone: +44 (0) 1243 771107 or email: enquiries@summersdale.com.

HOW TO READ
the
Universe

HOW TO UNDERSTAND SIGNS, SYNCHRONICITY AND OTHER COSMIC CLUES

ASTRID CARVEL

summersdale

Contents

Welcome

Congratulations on taking your first steps to understanding the language of the universe!

Through paying attention to the subtle (and sometimes not so subtle) signs the universe is constantly sending, you'll find that the cosmos is gifting you the keys to a happier, healthier and more fulfilled life.

From providing you with clarity on your path to living with a more mindful and self-reflective approach, you'll gain a greater understanding of yourself and your place in the world. You'll also improve connections with others in your life (they're part of the universe too!) and open doors to significant connections and opportunities that you might otherwise miss.

Signs from the universe can take many forms and your interpretation can depend on the significance you assign to different experiences and perceptions. Every sign is meant for you alone and depends on your unique needs and desires at that moment. For example, finding a white feather on the way home when you've just missed out on a job promotion may alert you to a message from your guardian angel. It may be that they're offering you comfort or letting you know that something better is on the way. To someone else, their situation may be different and the feather may have another meaning, or they may attach no meaning to it at all.

This book explores some of the most common signs from the universe and their meanings, then encourages you to add and interpret your own signs in the fill-in section at the end. With a little cosmic luck, getting to grips with the language of the universe might ultimately help you to lead a more intuitive, meaningful existence. Wishing you joy, discovery and enlightenment on your journey!

Chapter One

What are signs from the
UNIVERSE?

Have you ever seen the most beautiful butterfly right at the moment when you were thinking of a loved one who has passed on? This chapter introduces us to the wonder of signs from the universe: what they are and how our understanding of them has grown over the last 70 years.

With insights from the founder of analytical psychology Carl Jung and US talk-show queen Oprah Winfrey, we'll look at the meaning of the terms "synchronicity" and "paying attention" to understand how we can apply these concepts to reading the universe. We'll also learn about how the universe works energetically, how to ask it for a sign and how to spot and interpret these signs in ways that will make our hearts sing.

Synchronicity is an ever-present reality for those who have eyes to see.

Carl Jung

What is synchronicity?

Has a song ever popped into your head only for you to hear it on the radio a minute later? Or perhaps you were thinking of a particular person when suddenly your phone rang and the screen lit up with their name?

According to the Swiss psychiatrist Carl Jung, these are examples of synchronicity, or "meaningful coincidences". Jung first coined the term in 1952 in his book *Synchronicity: An Acausal Connecting Principle*. In it he describes synchronicities as seemingly coincidental yet meaningful events in the world around us that do not have an obvious cause.

Jung believed that many "coincidences" were not down to chance but instead related to our thoughts becoming reality – much in the same way we talk about "manifestation" today. These signs from the universe could provide powerful insight, direction and guidance, awakening the individual to their full potential and allowing them to make true connections with their inner self.

What's the purpose of synchronicity?

✦ **Spiritualists** believe synchronicity is a sign from their higher self or soul, guiding them on the right path through life and spiritual awakening.

✦ **Quantum physicists** attribute synchronicity to universal consciousness, or the idea that there is one universal mind. This idea dates back 2,500 years to the Greek philosopher Anaxagoras, who formulated the cosmological theory of nous (Greek for "mind"), describing one universal mind that controls everything in the universe. This suggests an underlying essence to all things – one single consciousness pervading the entire universe.

✦ **Psychologists**, particularly those who follow Jungian theories, believe synchronicity comes from the unconscious mind and collective unconscious (meaning the unconscious common to humankind as a whole). Jung believed that this idea explained why similar themes crop up in mythologies worldwide. He argued that the life of every individual is profoundly influenced by the unconscious mind, which is why we attribute meaning to symbols based on our experiences.

- ✦ **Behavioural economists** see synchronicity as a form of confirmation bias, which is the tendency to search for information in a way that confirms your own beliefs and values. For example, if your brain tells you to look for red cars, you'll start seeing a lot more of them!

- ✦ **Sceptics** think synchronicity is simply seeing connections and patterns in random and/or meaningless data (known as "apophenia").

Many people believe that synchronicity is a thumbs-up from the universe to tell us we're on the right track about something. These instances seem far too significant to be mere coincidences. Some even describe them as miracles, signs from the heavens, guidance from a personal spirit guide or a mystical instance of soul connection. How exciting to know that every time you meet someone new, there might be an element of synchronicity that's helping you on your journey!

How can I recognize synchronicity?

Once you get to know the signs, you'll begin to see them everywhere! Here are some examples of synchronicity:

✦ Spontaneous encounters, for example meeting a potential business contact in the queue at the grocery store.

✦ Prophetic dreams/visions or repeatedly noticing details from dreams in real life.

✦ Seeing shapes or patterns (like in cloud formations) or frequently spotting the same shape.

✦ Noticing recurring symbols that are meaningful to you, such as certain colours or flowers.

✦ Continually seeing the same number, or sequence of numbers, time and time again.

✦ Receiving a message, for example a reassuring text, when you most need it.

✦ Hearing a certain song, or opening a book at a page that speaks directly to you.

✦ Thinking about something, only for it to mysteriously happen.

✦ Being in the right place at the right time.

How to improve your ability to recognize synchronicity

According to Jung, there are two ways to do this:

1   By being mindful and paying more attention to our surroundings (see "Paying attention" on page 23).

2   By developing the analytical skills to consider what events might mean. One of the most useful ways to improve your analytical skills is through journalling (see page 131 for more information about journalling).

Once you follow Jung's tips, you'll become more familiar with the types of signs the universe is sending your way!

What's the difference between serendipity and synchronicity?

Good question! Serendipity is a single experience of good fortune. For example, you may get to the checkout in the store only to find you've left your wallet at home. Then, fishing around in your pocket, you find some cash you didn't know was there.

Meanwhile, synchronicity refers to (often recurring) events or signs that are highly symbolic and meaningful to you.

Universal energy

Let's look at how universal energy creates synchronicity:

Albert Einstein proved that everything in our universe is made up of energy, from the chair you're sitting on to the stars you see twinkling at night. This energy constantly flows and changes form, and it lasts forever, so it can't be created or destroyed. Universal energy sustains life by providing vital sustenance to all living systems, such as the energy sunlight gives to plants.

Life force energy is all around us and, whether we can see it or not, it's an indisputable part of our existence. Our thoughts, emotions and actions come from this source. By consciously tapping into this energy, we can bring enormous healing, grounding, personal power and synchronicity into our lives, helping us to reach our full potential and achieve our higher purpose on Earth.

Vibrations

The concepts of vibration and frequency can help us to understand the law of attraction more fully: everything is energy, energy is constantly moving, and everything has its own vibration (including us). We are each spinning whirlpools of interactive energy with our own unique energy signature. Different energies vibrate at different frequencies, so we will attract things or people vibrating at a similar frequency to ourselves.

Our experiences, thoughts and emotions also have a vibrational frequency. In order to prevent negative things from entering our lives, we need to change our frequencies to attract something more desirable. We have to make ourselves a vibrational match to our goal, so that "like can attract like".

What or who would you like to attract into your life, and how might you change your current thoughts or behaviours in order to become more of a match to that person or thing?

Signs that you're good at reading universal energy

Some people are more naturally sensitive to the energies given out by the universe than others. Check the signs below to see how many of them resonate with you:

☐ You're sensitive to the emotional states of others

☐ You experience a sense of discomfort in crowded places because you find the energies of so many people in one room overwhelming

☐ You're seeking spiritual connection with others – you'd love to find or expand your group of like-minded friends

☐ You have very vivid dreams

☐ You're keen on spiritual development

☐ You have a continuous search for purpose

☐ You have strong intuition and it's often correct

☐ You're able to manifest your desires

How did you score?

0–2: Your receptivity to universal energy is currently low, but don't despair! Help is at hand on the very next page with tips on how to develop and nurture your sensitivity to universal energy. You'll become more aware of the signs the universe may be sending you in no time!

3–5: You have a good level of sensitivity to universal energy but there is room for improvement and you may still be missing some of the signs the universe is trying to send you.

6–8: You have a highly empathic nature and find it relatively easy to read the universe and connect with others. Continue to deepen your connection to your soul and spirituality so that you'll be able to read even more signs from the universe!

How to develop your sensitivity to universal energy

1   Start by writing down your dreams in a dream journal and look for repeating patterns. This will develop your ability to interpret your dreams and see their relevance to your life.

2   Dedicate some time to meditation, ideally in nature when possible. This will help you feel part of the universe and connected with the energy of all living things.

3   Stargazing – or watching the sky during daylight hours – is an excellent way to feel connected to the universe.

4   Learn about the different lunar phases and take notice of your changing emotional states during them, as well as the different seasons of the year.

5   Raise your vibrational frequency by engaging in an energizing activity, such as sitting in the sun or dancing. Feel that energy shimmy through you!

The law of attraction

Just like universal energy, the law of attraction is always in action too. Since vibrations attract similar vibrational frequency, the law of attraction literally means "like attracts like" and determines your ability to attract the things you desire. This means that anything you can imagine is possible, as long as you take steps in the right direction. Once you launch the thought and take action, the universe will step in to meet you halfway.

Those who believe in the law of attraction believe that, with every moment and every thought of your life, you're consciously creating your own reality. If you're plagued by negative thoughts, you may unintentionally attract your worst fears to come true. If you focus on positive thoughts, set goals and take steps to achieve them, then this is what you will manifest.

So, if you focus on paying attention to cosmic signs, guess what? You'll attract more of them!

Manifestation

Are you desperate to find a new job, one that makes the most of your talents and gives you satisfaction? Or perhaps you're looking for a loving and enduring relationship? Our desires can range from life-changing ones like these to smaller aspirations, such as winning a baking competition at work.

Manifesting your desires involves intentionally visualizing what you want and bringing it into your reality, and it has become increasingly popular. This can be achieved through positive thoughts, emotions and feelings that send the right energy out into the universe. Using what we know about universal energy, vibrations and the law of attraction can help our manifesting power.

And, of course, we can always ask the universe for synchronicities to let us know we're on the right track with our manifestation.

Paying attention

American TV personality and spiritual innovator Oprah Winfrey believes that we all need to pay attention to what the universe is telling us. She believes that she manifested being cast in the role of Sofia in the 1985 film *The Color Purple* and says that by "paying attention" we can check in with what we're manifesting in our lives, whether consciously or unconsciously.

Oprah believes there are many things in life that we have control over if we pay attention. She has said, "You are sleepwalking through your life." She recommends actively listening to the "whispers" in life and paying attention to every single experience: "They're telling you something."

In multiple interviews, Oprah shared the question she wishes everyone would ask themselves: "Why didn't you pay attention to your life?" Ask yourself now if there any areas of your life that you need to pay attention to.

What if you don't listen?

Most of us will have experienced the feeling of a situation becoming worse, such as a toxic friendship spiralling out of control. In some instances, we may have been ignoring signs about something we just didn't want to face. The universe will let you know when it's time to make a change – or take a stand!

Ignore the signs at your peril, advises Oprah. If you're tuned in and paying attention, you'll hear a whisper and can then respond accordingly. If you ignore the whisper, Oprah warns that it will transform into a pebble thumping on your head. If this happens, you may be in trouble – but there's still time to fix it!

Oprah says that if you continue to ignore the signs, the pebble turns into a brick (a crisis) pounding on your head, the brick wall will crumble and your whole house will collapse. So, we'd all be well advised to heed those whispers from the universe!

How to manifest

Here are some tips on how to begin manifesting:

1   You have to match your vibrational frequency to the vibration of the thing you want.

2   In order to attract your goal or desire to you, don't let fear of not getting it block your path.

3   Put your intention out to the universe, either by speaking it aloud or writing it down, then let it go.

4   Always do your groundwork to make sure you're prepared for when your opportunity arrives. Let go of any attachment to receiving your desire, but be ready for when it shows up – and remember to say thank you.

If you're not caught up in what Oprah calls your "small personality mind" – meaning the fears and constraints of your ego – you'll find you're paying much more attention to the present moment and, therefore, to your life. This means you create a clearer channel for the universe's messages and your desires to reach you.

How to ask the universe for a sign

Just remember to ask!

1   Think of a question you'd like the answer to and phrase it as clearly as you can so there's no room for confusion.

2   Frame your request as a yes–no question. This makes it simpler to interpret what you receive.

3   Trust that you'll receive an answer and then consciously let go. It's important to surrender control to the universe as it always knows what's best.

4   As you go about your day, be in the present moment and pay attention to anything that draws your interest. Look for patterns, recurring numbers or themes, or even just a single image or word that seems to stand out to you even if you don't realize why!

5   Express gratitude. Once you've received guidance, it's important to say thank you.

Alternative ways to ask

If you feel more comfortable writing your request, note it down and spend a few moments thinking about the question you're asking. Then put it away in a drawer and consider your request sent. Remember to return later and note the answer you've been given so that you can see how the universe communicates with you.

If you think you might struggle to identify signs:

1   Ask for a clear sign within a specific timeframe. For example, within the next 24 or 48 hours.

2   Specify what you want your sign to be and pick something unusual that you wouldn't normally see. If you do see it, it will be an obvious message.

You'll know you're in tune with the universe when you receive your desire. If you don't receive it, question your motivation. The universe may be telling you that somehow you're not on the right track.

How to interpret synchronicity

Something strange just happened and you think it may be a sign from the universe – what should you do now? Here are some of the best ways to experience synchronicity:

1   **Immerse yourself in the present moment:** Be alert to all that you're feeling and sensing in this moment to gather as many clues as you can.

2   **Tap into your senses:** This includes all five of your senses, as well as your "sixth sense", your intuition (for more on this, see Chapter Five). Notice any scents or sounds that surround the synchronicity, or any intuitive feeling that you get, and write these down afterwards when you're considering the meaning of your cosmic sign.

3   **Meditate and go inwards:** Ask yourself, "What does this synchronicity mean to me?" Take note of any images, feelings or words that enter your head.

4   **Tune into your body:** Your body holds much wisdom and knows the truth, despite what your mind might lead you to believe. When you think about what your synchronicity might mean, see if you get a warm feeling or any shivers or goosebumps. If you do, it's likely you've found the right explanation for what your sign means. However, if you can't feel any discernible changes in your body, keep looking, as you probably haven't found the answer yet.

Always remember to consider what something means to you. While you can look up reliable online guidance, your personal interpretation is the only one that counts. Correctly interpreting the signs that appear in your life can help you to know when you're on the right path and living in alignment with your deepest desires, needs and values.

Tips to manifest signs and synchronicity into your life

If you're looking for ways to start manifesting synchronicity, try some of the following tips. The good news is there are lots of different approaches to try:

✦ Be open-minded to receiving cosmic signs. Because of the law of attraction, believing in the signs and being open to how they appear will help you to manifest them more. The result may not be in a form that you expected, but it could be better than you imagined.

✦ Take a moment to consider what you'd like to achieve in your life. Make sure your intentions are pure, heartfelt and not intended to cause harm to anyone else. Intentionally direct your thoughts and energy towards what's important to you and the universe will respond. Be specific in your intentions and be clear about why you want to receive signals from the universe. Perhaps you'd like the universe to affirm that you're pursuing the right career path, or maybe you're looking for guidance when you have an important choice to make.

✦   Increase your awareness of your environment, as well as your own feelings and desires, in order to become more in tune with yourself and the universe.

✦   Trust that synchronicity will appear in your life and, when it does, trust your intuition to follow what's presented to you. When you learn to trust yourself, you learn to accept whatever is unfolding in your life at any moment.

✦   You don't have to be religious to experience the power of prayer. Ask to receive synchronicity from whatever source you believe in. You can express your desire verbally or mentally.

✦   Maintain a grateful, positive and clear outlook whenever you can to remain open and receptive in body and mind.

Cleansing your aura and balancing your chakras

As energetic beings, we are surrounded by an unseen spiritual energy field, known as an aura. You may have noticed how some people seem to bring you down and drain your vibrational energy while others lift you up with their bright, shiny auras. Your energy field often absorbs negative vibes from the environment and the people you come into contact with, and this can get in the way of your ability to tap into universal energy and pick up on cosmic signs.

Humans also have seven main chakras which are the body's energy centres and are connected to life force energy (you may have heard this referred to as *chi* or *prana*). Your chakras are a reflection of how your spiritual energy field is functioning. When they're in harmony with universal energy, you feel great. But if something's off balance, your well-being may be affected and you can end up feeling lost.

By investing in your health and wellness, you can take steps to heal your energetic vibrations. It can also feel empowering to show yourself some love and care. Try introducing some of the activities below into your regular schedule:

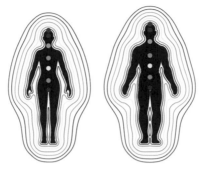

✦ **Meditation:** Even 5 minutes of this mindful practice can work wonders when it comes to balancing your energy, and there are many guided meditations available online to help get you started.

✦ **Sound baths:** Listening to particular frequencies and bathing in sound waves can be deeply immersive and healing.

✦ **Reiki or crystal healing:** For when you're out of balance, these ancient healing techniques help to cleanse negative energy and channel positivity.

✦ **Self-care:** The small but essential ways in which you care for your mind, body and soul help you to feel calm, grounded and in control. Practices can include taking a bath with aromatherapy candles, going for a woodland walk or cuddling with your (or someone else's) pet.

Figuring out how the universe communicates with you

✦ **Keep a journal** of the questions you ask the universe along with a record of the synchronicities or answers you receive.

✦ **Note the pattern.** You may see a pattern in the way the universe communicates with you. For example, some of us are more receptive to messages when they come through other people or animal visitations. How does the universe like to communicate with you?

✦ **The universe will play to your strengths.** If you're a visual person, you'll receive the sign as a visual image. If you're a people person, the universe may send you a message through a chance encounter with an old friend.

Gratitude

Expressing gratitude sends out positive energy to the universe and, due to the law of attraction, this means it will send you that love right back!

You can create something called a gratitude loop, which is an unlimited cycle of positive energy created by your gratitude – so next time you come to manifest your desires, the universe will send cosmic signs your way. On the other hand, forgetting to thank the universe for helping you can break this stream of positivity and you may be headed back to square one next time you're looking to manifest.

A gratitude journal is a great way to send out positive energy. Write down three things you're grateful for each day, or simply think about them before you go to bed. Doing this as part of your night-time routine will send you off to dreamland in a cloud of positive energy.

Chapter Two

ANGELS and SPIRIT GUIDES

Have you ever felt like someone was looking out for you when the perfect job landed in your lap, or when you escaped a potentially risky situation unscathed? If so, you may have been protected or guided by a divine messenger.

This chapter looks at signs from angels and spirit guides, exploring the gifts they bring and how they can assist us in unlocking the secrets of the universe. We'll explore the different types of spiritual guardians, the style of guidance they might send us and how to connect with them in order to ask for those all-important signs – their favourite way to communicate with us.

Once you embrace your angels and spirit guides, you'll open yourself up to beautiful and supportive friendships. Their wisdom can lift you higher and help you to channel positivity and find your purpose.

Ask for help from your angels, and trust that your team of guides and angels will help you as you take each and every step on your path.

Melanie Beckler

What are angels and spirit guides?

Angels exist to offer guidance and protection, while spirit guides are said to support our spiritual advancement.

Angels

When we think of angels, we often think of something fluttery with wings and a beautiful, bright energy. An angel is technically defined as a "spiritual being" who delivers messages on behalf of a god or deity and serves as an intermediary between this god and humans. They are thought to have protective qualities and be able to guide us on behalf of the divine.

Spirit guides

We all have a "spirit team" on our side. "Spirit guide" is an umbrella term referring to spiritual or celestial beings that can come from either human or non-human origins. They are said to occupy the spiritual realm alongside angels and are full of ancient wisdom that they are more than happy to share.

Common signs of an angel's visit

Unlike some other spirit guides, angels rarely communicate directly by voice, but they love to communicate through signs. Here are some of the most common ones:

✦ **Finding white feathers:** Has a feather ever floated down in front of you just as you're about to sit an exam or go to an important meeting? Seeing or finding a white feather is one of the most well-known and delightful angel signs. It tells you that an angel has heard your prayer and is offering protection, love, support or encouragement. Birds are a symbol of freedom and flight, and your angel's wings are too.

✦ **Rainbows:** These beautiful phenomena are said to be symbols of divine love, and angels can appear in this form to remind you that you're loved and that better things are on the way.

✦ **Recurring numbers:** Angels must have loved maths at universe school because they love communicating through numbers! Noticing the same number over and over or a repeating number sequence (such as 1111) is one of their common signs.

- ✦ **Dreams:** When you're asleep you're at your most relaxed, which means your subconscious mind is more open to receiving messages. Take note of any recurring themes or images that pop up in your dreams, as this may be one of your angels trying to tell you something significant.

- ✦ **Advertisements and billboards:** Being adept at moving with the times, angels often use ads to communicate. Catching your attention is precisely what an angel is hoping to do, so what better way than shouting it out from a large billboard?

- ✦ **Books or magazines:** Have you ever been taken by surprise when a book has fallen off the shelf or off a table? If this happens, open the book at a random page to see if it holds a message that resonates with you.

Angels and vibrations

Angels naturally vibrate at a much higher frequency than the earthly world. Coming into contact with an angel will raise your vibrations and amplify your energetic field. This can manifest itself as physical feelings in the body, for example the hairs on your arms might stand on end.

You may have the sensation of being touched, which most people feel on the top of their head, but it can happen anywhere on your body. This is where your crown chakra is located – your link to the divine.

Angels may also contact you through sound vibrations. If you get a ringing in your ears that sounds like buzzing or bells, it's thought that an angel is trying to deliver you a message that you're not ready to hear. They're "downloading" their guidance for your mind to translate at the right time.

Feeling or "sensing" an angel's presence

Sometimes the sign you receive from an angel may not be visual but will be a feeling or sensation, or involve another of your senses. You may experience the following:

✦ An overwhelming feeling of peace or love.

✦ A feeling of comfort that appears from nowhere when you're struggling with grief or despair.

✦ A sudden realization of what to do regarding a decision or situation.

✦ The feeling of a healing energy working within you that came out of nowhere.

✦ Tingling sensations or goosebumps.

✦ Butterflies in your stomach. Angels may be connecting with you through your solar plexus – your chakra centre of personal power – in order to help you make a decision about something.

✦ A feeling of warmth moving through your body.

✦ Scents. Guardian angels (protective spirits) have sometimes been described as having the smell of mint chocolate, while archangels are associated with a light floral scent.

Why might you see angel signs?

Angels may appear without you calling them for the following reasons:

✦ You may be going through a process of healing at the time you see an angel sign. Angels may appear to reassure you of their gentle support and encouragement.

✦ You may be feeling low or disconnected. Your angels want you to know that you're unconditionally loved and supported.

✦ They may be giving you a sign that you're following the right path and moving towards your purpose and authentic self.

✦ If you're going through a spiritual awakening, you may notice angel signs popping up all over the place. Your connection with the spirit realm and universe will be deepening and you'll start to see the world in more colours and dimensions than ever before. As your vibration rises, the beings you're able to connect with will be of higher vibrations.

Pythagoras and angel numbers

You may be surprised to know that the famous Greek philosopher Pythagoras (570–495 BCE) believed that numbers carried energetic vibrations and were the key to a spiritual life. Pythagoras saw everything in the universe as mathematically precise, believing that each number had its own vibration and meaning and that the order in which a sequence of numbers occurred was not random but significant.

So, the idea of our reality as a physical manifestation of energetic vibrations is as old as time. Yet the term "angel numbers" – the divining of a message from a number or sequence – was coined only this century by the author Doreen Virtue. Interpreting number sequences has now become a popular way of cracking the codes from your angel messengers.

In Pythagorean numerology, two numbers have the highest vibrational potential: 11 and 22. These are called **master numbers** and were thought by Pythagoras to be associated with revelation.

Angel numbers

Have you ever looked at your watch or phone and noticed that the time is exactly 11:11? And then done exactly the same thing the next day? Repetitive number sequences that keep catching your attention are known as angel numbers and are said to be messages from your winged helpers.

You'll find some general meanings associated with each number on the next page, but whenever you see a particular sequence recurring it's always important to ask your angels what they are trying to tell you. Listen to your thoughts, feelings and dreams in order to hear their response and gain clues as to what the message may be.

Seeing angel numbers is like a reassuring hug from your heavenly team. They want you to know that you're doing great and to offer their guidance to help you get to where you want to be.

Interpreting angel numbers

When you interpret signs from angels, spirit guides or any other divine source, you should always pay attention to your own intuition and the personal meaning something may have to you. Your intuition will always be your best guidance system (see Chapter Five).

To develop your own understanding of the numbers, try the following:

1   Make a note of the number or recurring number sequence that seems to have been popping up everywhere lately.

2   Write down next to it any thoughts, emotions or impressions that come to mind when you see or think of that number.

The more you formulate your own understanding of what the numbers mean personally to you and the vibrations you pick up from them, the easier it will be next time a particular number shows up for you in the future.

Angel number meanings

Angel numbers can help you to make sense of life experiences and give you valuable insight on a current situation. Or they might be saying, "Congratulations, you're on the right path!"

Meaningful digits can be repeated individually or can appear within a pattern:

✦ **0:** Zero indicates that there's a fresh start coming for you. As you start this new cycle of your life, don't be shy of being a revolutionary and creating the life that you truly desire.

✦ **1:** One is a powerful manifestation figure, so be sure to manifest something positive.

✦ **2:** Two represents balance and alignment. You're receiving help to get you where you need to go, so trust and go with it.

✦ **3:** Three is the number of creative fire! It encourages you to follow your innate gifts and passions.

- ✦ **4:** Four is about stability. It means you're building the foundations to achieve your desires.

- ✦ **5:** Five suggests major changes are on the way, but this is for the best and will align you with your correct path.

- ✦ **6:** Six is a compassionate number and a reminder to treat yourself with kindness and understanding. Know that if things don't go to plan, everything happens for a reason.

- ✦ **7:** Seven can bring good news for your finances, or it may be asking you to take notice of your internal world and develop your spirituality.

- ✦ **8:** Eight encourages you to follow your intuition. It's the symbol of infinity and some believe that they're receiving support from departed loved ones when they see this number.

- ✦ **9:** Nine is often related to endings, but these are nothing to be feared. A new cycle is imminent, so dig deep and think about what you truly want to create, knowing the universe has your back.

Archangels

Archangels are said to be made of pure love. While they are traditionally thought of in Christianity as being the highest-ranking angels in Heaven, they are actually in the second lowest rank according to ancient theological texts. This is because they need to be close to humankind to deliver messages and guidance from the divine.

The word "archangel" is derived from the Greek arche ("ruler") and angelos ("messenger") showing their dual role: they rule over other angels but also deliver messages to humankind.

The number of archangels is debated among different faiths, but it's generally accepted that there are seven main archangels, each specializing in a particular area. Every archangel supervises their own team of angels, and these teams are each associated with a different colour and work on one of seven light ray frequencies. Every colour has its own energy vibration, and so any recurring colours you notice may be a giveaway as to which archangel is trying to communicate with you.

The seven main archangels are:

MICHAEL

The leader of the archangels and a spiritual warrior you can call on for protection.

Colour: Blue

Key words: Protection, faith, courage, strength, power

GABRIEL

The famous "Messenger" (or "Angel of Revelation") helps you to understand the messages you receive. So if you're a bit baffled, you can call on Gabriel to help you interpret your cosmic sign.

Colour: White

Key words: Purity, harmony, holiness

RAPHAEL

"The Healer", who can also help with prosperity.
Colour: Green
Key words: Healing, prosperity

URIEL

"The Transformer", sharing wisdom, illuminating truth and offering support during change.
Colour: Red
Key words: Wisdom, service

ARIEL

The archangel of nature.
Colour: Pink
Key words: Love, peace

CHAMUEL

"The Nurturer", cultivating self-love and love of others.
Colour: Purple
Key words: Transformation, mercy

ZADKIEL

"The Forgiver", Zadkiel helps with compassion and forgiveness.
Colour: Yellow
Key words: Wisdom for making decisions

Asking archangels for signs

Try the following if you'd like to receive signs from an archangel:

1   Find a quiet place, and focus on your heart centre. Ask for whatever archangel is appropriate for you at this particular moment to show you a sign. Archangels may use typical angel signs or you may see or notice a particular colour. You may see a flash of colour itself or notice a striking coloured object that is somehow out of place. Some people claim to have seen a blue orb or sparks when they have felt Archangel Michael near, for example.

2   You can also contact specific archangels by actively working with the colours they're associated with. Some people find a nice way to do this is with coloured candles. If there's an area in your life you'd like help with – for example, love – then you could light a pink candle to connect with Archangel Ariel. When you light the candle, focus on the colour. As you start to feel yourself connecting with that archangel's light ray, say your question or ask for a sign to guide you with regards to a specific issue.

It's useful to keep an open mind when asking angels for signs or guidance. Angels have a wonderful sense of humour and can deliver what you need in many ways, and some of them may be unexpected! Sometimes angels will also work through professionals around you, such as when you see a specialist doctor for your particular condition.

Angels work to their own timescale, but you may receive signs as quickly as within a week of your request.

In what other ways might archangels appear?

An angel's favourite method of communication is through the use of signs, but some people say they can feel an angel's energy, see a colour, glow or apparition, and some claim to have physically seen a vision of an archangel.

Archangels have traditionally been thought of as male, but this could be because they were recorded in ancient texts as male by default. Some modern believers conceive angels to exist beyond gender, as beings of the spiritual realm where gender is said not to exist. Others see some angels, such as Jophiel the archangel of beauty and wisdom, as having feminine energies.

Perhaps the most important thing to consider is that angels and archangels may appear in human or heavenly form, depending on what will be recognized by their human so that their message will be received. A passer-by who popped up in your hour of need and then disappeared without a trace could have been an angel in human form.

The four best known archangels (Michael, Gabriel, Raphael and Uriel) can make themselves known via tarot cards or signs relating to a compass point or element. The four compass points and four natural elements (Earth, Fire, Air and Water) are said to keep us in balance.

Tarot cards

These are the cards each archangel is associated with:

Archangel Michael: Temperance
Meaning: Balance, harmony and the connection of the spiritual and physical realms.

Archangel Gabriel: Judgement
Meaning: Spiritual communication, awakenings and resurrections.

Archangel Raphael: The Lovers
Meaning: Connecting with soul mates, heart healing, romantic and platonic.

Archangel Uriel: The Devil
Meaning: Sheds light on the illusions which keep us trapped, helping us to grow and learn from our mistakes.

Elements

If you receive any signs related to compass point directions or the below elements, an Archangel may be trying to send you a message:

Earth/North: Archangel Uriel

Fire/South: Archangel Michael

Air/East: Archangel Raphael

Water/West: Archangel Gabriel

Guardian angels

Most of us have had experiences where we've felt that someone, somewhere was watching over us. Perhaps we inexplicably walked away from an accident without a scratch or fell into a career path we weren't expecting but came to love. Our guardian angels protect us from harm and guide us on our life's path. While beliefs differ as to how many of them we each have, it's generally agreed that everyone has at least one blessing us for a whole lifetime.

Guardian angels aren't physically visible to most humans for good reason – so you don't jump out of your skin in alarm if you see one or feel constantly watched. They don't want to frighten or distract us as we go about our lives because that would hinder our spirit's experience. But just because you can't see them, doesn't mean they're not there and ready to leap to your aid.

Signs from your guardian angel

Like humans, guardian angels have their own distinctive personalities – so you're likely to experience signs unique and meaningful to you and your angel. They'll know what you're thinking, what makes you laugh, as well as the things that make you sit up and take notice. Once you work with them, you'll begin to see their personalities – they already know yours!

Asking your guardian angel for a sign

If you'd like help from your guardian angel – or even just confirmation of their reassuring presence – you can ask for a sign. You can do this through prayer or meditation, by writing to them or by playing a specific song. Experts in angelology (the study of angels) agree that the most important thing is to ask – but the way you choose is up to you. So, get chatting and interacting – it's the best way to get to know your guardian angels!

Easy steps for getting to know your guardian angel

Having a positive relationship with your guardian angel can offer you support in both good and tough times, and help you chart a smoother course through life. These easy suggestions can help you to get to know your guardian angel and become familiar with their method of communication:

Find out their name

When you first connect with your guardian angel, make sure you're in a quiet space with a clear mind, such as during meditation. Ask for the name of your guardian angel, either aloud or in your mind. The name should then pop into your head. If you don't receive anything, your guardian angel could be encouraging you to name them yourself! Choose a name that makes you feel warm inside.

Write the name of yours here:

My guardian angel is called: ....

Ask questions

The more confident you become at asking your guardian angel questions and interpreting the answers, the better you'll understand each other.

Ask your angel specific questions that you need help with, for example, "How can I improve my relationship with my partner?" The answer may arrive in your head immediately or you may be given a sign a few days later. If you don't receive anything after about a week, give your angel the benefit of the doubt – they may not know the answer or it could be something they're not allowed to reveal to you for a reason you're not aware of. Perhaps a sign will be revealed to you when you're ready to receive it.

If you think you've received a sign from your guardian angel but you haven't a clue what it means, ruminate on it for a while then ask for clarification. You can even ask how they prefer to communicate or share your own preference.

Types of spirit guides

Spirit guides can originate from many sources, ranging from extra-terrestrial systems and the divine to those who have lived on Earth. If you're not sure which spirit guides you might have on your team, it doesn't matter. A good indicator is which type you feel most connected to, but you'll soon get to know them. Here are some well-known categories of guides:

✦ **Ascended masters:** Former human souls who have spiritually ascended and no longer have the need to reincarnate on Earth. Famous examples include Jesus, Buddha, Mother Mary, Guanyin (a former Buddhist princess) and Merlin. Healers or those who are spiritually awakened often work with these.

✦ **Saints**

✦ **Starseeds:** Beings from other star systems, planets or galaxies who have incarnated on Earth to help humankind.

✦ **Elementals:** Nature spirits.

✦ **Ancestors:** See page 65.

✦ **Goddesses or other deities**

✦ **Spirit animals:** See page 82.

How many spirit guides do you have?

The answer: you have a whole team! And you may not even know they're there or what each is doing behind the scenes. Some of them are with us for life, but often a variety of them will come and go during your time on Earth. They will work with you as and when you need them and they each have different specialities and knowledge. For example, you may have a guide to help you through the lessons of a romantic relationship, and if and when that relationship ends, the guide will leave. They will usually help you overcome a specific issue, attain a particular achievement or fulfil a distinct purpose.

How to contact your spirit guide

Try this spirit guide meditation:

1   Make yourself comfortable somewhere quiet where you won't be disturbed.

2   Play some relaxing music and clear your mind of mental chatter.

3   Once you feel your mind clear, ask your guide to step forward. You may see or intuit your guide with your third eye*, or you may sense them.

4   You can ask for your guide's name and how they're here to help you. Let them know about anything that you'd like specific assistance with. Listen objectively to any advice they give.

* The third eye or brow chakra is located in the middle of your forehead. It's believed to be the centre of intuition and perception and it allows you to see beyond the realms of ordinary sight and deepen your spiritual connection.

5   Ask your guide for a physical sign, like the appearance of a specific object or word, number or type of animal. Or you can ask them to give you a symbol or image that is to be associated with them.

6   Always remember to thank them afterwards.

Other methods of connection include:

✦   Walking in nature or keeping a clear head and energy field will mean you're more receptive to your guide's energies.

✦   Asking your guide to appear to you in a dream, and being open-minded about how they may appear. They could be as small as a woodlouse or as important as a queen. Each has an important and specific message, so pay attention!

✦   Some guides like to work through tools, such as runes or angel cards.

What signs might you receive from a spirit guide?

✦ Seeing your guide in your mind's eye, or a symbol associated uniquely with them that you would recognize.

✦ Receiving a gut feeling or intuition.

✦ Feeling suddenly calm during a moment of turmoil.

✦ Feeling a presence with you or a sudden uplift in spirits when you had been feeling sad, lonely or upset.

✦ Like angels, guides may visit you through dreams.

✦ Spirit guides often like to drop ideas or messages into your head. You may even hear them "speaking".

✦ Signs in media such as TV, music or books.

✦ Physical assistance or words of wisdom from other humans.

If a presence or form of communication feels familiar, this could be a deceased relative who wants to offer you guidance. Read more about ancestor guides on the next page.

Ancestor guides

Have you ever felt like you're being watched over by a much-loved grandparent who passed away? It's common for ancestors from any preceding generation to want to help younger family members make their way in life. These spirits are known as ancestor guides.

Many cultures still carry out ancient rituals where they commune with their ancestors and revere them as guides. For example, Vodun worshippers in West Africa believe the souls of the dead walk among the living at certain times and perform the annual ceremony of dancing Egunguns (or "living ghosts") as an ancestral rite.

Although some traditions keep the skulls of their ancestors to chat to, tamer methods include:

✦ Connecting through meditation.

✦ Making food, art or music that you dedicate to your ancestors.

✦ Performing ritual ceremonies and festivities.

✦ Thinking of them, asking for their guidance or talking to them in your head when going about your daily business.

Communicating with ancestors is a wonderful way to keep their spirit alive – and lift yours.

Chapter Three
SYMBOLS

The universe speaks to us using symbols, which are imbued with meaning. The significance these symbols carry is often loaded with traditional and ancient cultural resonance, but remember to always consider what a symbol means to you personally.

This chapter looks at some of the most common symbols: traditional shapes that make up the physical landscape of the universe (such as triangles, squares and circles), as well as clouds, recurring colours, animal visitations and many other objects that are often used by the universe to get our attention.

On your journey, perhaps you'll discover some favourite symbols that have special significance just for you.

Coins

Finding a coin on the ground or in another unlikely place is traditionally seen as an auspicious sign from the universe, yet most of us might be tempted to walk right on past. Here are some of the wonderful signals the universe could be giving us with that very coin:

Abundance

No matter how small, coins are one of the signs the universe sends as a symbol of abundance. Although it may only be a penny or cent, it reminds us that having gratitude for the seemingly insignificant things paves the way for receiving larger rewards. It's also good to remember that rewards come in many other forms than just financial.

Following the right path

Try and remember what you were thinking about at the time when you found the coin. This could be a sign that you're on the "right path" with something.

Sign from an angel or spirit guide

Many see a coin as a "message from Heaven". When sent from the angelic realm, the coin is believed to symbolize leadership and support. Spirit guides are also often said to leave coins, usually as guidance to help you make a decision. Both are likely to leave coins in unusual places in order to get your attention.

Other meanings

✦ A reminder that you're valued, loved and supported.

✦ A sign of new beginnings or positive change.

✦ A message from a loved one who has passed over, showing love and support.

✦ A symbol of good luck – some believe that finding pennies or cents is especially lucky!

So, next time you see a coin in a strange place, instead of walking past, pay attention and ask yourself: what was on your mind at the time you spotted the coin?

Objects

As well as coins, the universe can use any small, seemingly mundane object to catch your attention. It may choose something very specific that seems decidedly odd. This is because it wants the object to stand out to you, so think very carefully about any memories or feelings the object might evoke. Perhaps it's associated with a lovely memory of a favourite grandparent, or maybe a spirit guide is reminding you of a particular experience to point out something you need to work with and overcome. The object could be answering a question or it might be a sign supporting a new idea.

Losing/finding objects

We tend to develop attachments to our most treasured belongings, and the universe may use these to send us a message. If you've lost something, this may be the universe telling you to let go of the past. Ask yourself whether this object or something associated with it has been holding you back. When you find something that had gone missing, you may be reminded of meaningful associations with that item. Is the universe jogging your memory for a reason?

Breaking or malfunctioning objects

Something breaking at an inconvenient time can be incredibly frustrating – but this may actually be a sign that the universe has different intentions. Perhaps you need to go and buy a new oven, but what if you happen to have a chance encounter on the way that brings you a new partner or takes you a step forward in your career!

Technological malfunctions

The Wi-Fi going down (again) may make us want to scream, but could it in fact be a sign that you should reword or not send that email? Or perhaps the universe is telling you to take a break from your screen.

Clouds

Have you ever looked at the sky and seen a cloud in the shape of an animal, a heart, or even one that looks like an angel? Whatever shape appears, consider whether it might have special significance for you.

Many civilizations have viewed clouds as divine or supernatural, and their connection to rain symbolizes a life-giving energy. When Carl Jung spotted a person-shaped cloud, he pondered about its spiritual significance. He concluded that a person-shaped cloud was a reminder of our interconnectedness with the divine and reminded us to be open to the possibility of spiritual encounters.

If you see faces in the clouds, make a note of their expressions and think about how they make you feel and help you better understand your inner emotional state. If you see an animal, consider its inherent qualities and how you might direct that energy into your life.

Rainbows

Rainbows symbolize hope, new beginnings, good fortune, peace, spiritual growth, divinity, transformation, expansion and creation – and many people feel a deep connection to them. They also signify spiritual union in many cultures, and the rainbow is believed by some to bridge Heaven and Earth. While Vikings believed a burning rainbow bridge led their warriors to Valhalla, the Japanese told the story of the creators of the planet riding a rainbow to Earth and making land out of the ocean.

Many goddesses are also linked with the rainbow. In ancient Greek mythology, Iris, the messenger of the gods, was the rainbow in human form. In Chinese mythology, the creator goddess Nüwa patched the sky with stones of different colours after it had been torn apart by a war among divine creatures. For Buddhists, the rainbow is linked with enlightenment, representing the second highest level to be attained before nirvana.

Butterflies

Considered a special message from Heaven, butterflies are often seen as a sign from a departed loved one. These beautiful creatures are a symbol of transformation and transcendence – perhaps because their delicate wings remind us of angels and other celestial beings or the "flight" to the heavenly realm. They may also symbolize spiritual awakening because of the transformation from caterpillar to butterfly.

If a butterfly lands on you or flutters around you, it may be a loved one, angel or spirit guide letting you know that they are watching over you and that you are loved and protected. Whenever you see a butterfly, notice who or what it's reminding you of and mentally ask if it has a message for you. Don't worry if it doesn't – sometimes, you may instinctively know why the butterfly has been sent to you.

Recurring colours

Is there a certain colour that seems to be constantly grabbing your attention? Perhaps you've just walked into a room where you noticed red curtains, and then someone's handed you a red pen. Colours carry their own energy frequencies, and therefore are associated with particular meanings:

RED
Stability, passion, spontaneity, physical energy, vitality, stamina
Associated chakra: Root

ORANGE
Creativity, productivity, pleasure, warmth, enthusiasm, emotional expression, optimism
Associated chakra: Sacral

YELLOW
Personal power, fun, intellect, creativity, logic
Associated chakra: Solar plexus

GREEN
Love, harmony, balance, nature, acceptance
Associated chakra: Heart

BLUE
Communication, self-expression, peace, truth, tranquillity
Associated chakra: Throat

INDIGO
Intuition, perception, imagination, psychic abilities
Associated chakra: Third eye

PURPLE OR WHITE
Spiritual connection to the divine and higher realms, higher wisdom
Associated chakra: Crown

Flowers

For thousands of years, humans have gifted flowers to symbolize love, remembrance, friendship and celebration. Sometimes flowers are so meaningful to us that we dry or press them to preserve the memories they represent. As one of Mother Nature's greatest gifts, they are an ideal divination tool through which the cosmos can communicate with you.

Some common flower meanings include:

ROSE

In ancient mythology, the rose symbolizes love and adoration and is associated with Aphrodite, the Greek goddess of love. Specific colours carry certain meanings:

✦ Red: Love and romance

✦ Yellow: Friendship

✦ Orange: Enthusiasm and passion

✦ White: Sincerity, purity, innocence

✦ Pink: Gratitude, grace, admiration

SNOWDROP

One of the first flowers of spring, they symbolize hope, new beginnings and the ability to overcome challenges.

LILY

Love, devotion, purity, fertility and rebirth. Specific colours have special significance:

- ✦ White: Purity, virtue
- ✦ Pink (stargazer lily): Prosperity and abundance
- ✦ Red: Passion
- ✦ Orange (tiger lily): Confidence, pride and wealth
- ✦ Yellow: Gratitude and desire for enjoyment

DAFFODIL

Rebirth and new beginnings

GERBERA

Happiness

BLUEBELL

Humility, gratitude, constancy and everlasting love

Flower readings

Would you like a sign from the universe about a current situation? A flower reading could be the perfect way to receive the guidance you need.

Follow the steps below to do a flower reading:

1   First of all, select the flowers you wish to do the reading with. Do this intuitively, perhaps while looking at your garden or out walking, noting any that you find particularly appealing. Select up to five flowers. (There's no need to cut them and have them in front of you, unless you want to or are guided to).

2   Determine the name of each flower and look up the meaning of each (the internet is the perfect tool for this, although there are some common flower meanings on the previous pages).

3   Look up the meaning of the colours (see page 75).

4   Write down the meaning of each flower's colour and its symbolism in a journal and see if you begin to notice a pattern of what the flowers and colours represent.

5   Make note of any feelings, vibes, emotions or messages that you might be getting from your own intuition.

6   Each flower forms a part of the whole reading. Along with your intuitive hunches, try to tie everything together to divine one overall message.

White feathers

Feathers have been significant throughout history – from the Aztecs who wore quetzal feathers to symbolize status, to the people of Samoa and Tonga who used feathers as a currency. Although western cultures link white feathers with angels (as explored in Chapter Two), other beliefs also recognize them as a bridge between Earth and the spirit world, like some Indigenous American cultures. In ancient Egypt they were associated with the goddess Ma'at who signified truth, balance and justice.

Here are some other spiritual meanings associated with white feathers:

✦ Purity and new beginnings.

✦ Peace: The white feathers of the dove symbolize harmony and tranquillity.

✦ Good luck.

✦ Truth, divine justice and wisdom.

✦ Faith and hope: If you've been feeling a little lost, a white feather may be encouraging you to persist with your goals. You could be closer to achieving them than you think.

- ✦ Healing: The association of the white feather with healing links back to Ancient Rome (see the text box below). If you've been feeling a little unwell and you see a white feather, it could be a sign you're on the mend.

- ✦ Love: If you're looking for love and you find a white feather, you may be on to something. White feathers can also symbolize unconditional love from the divine, your angels or spirit guides, or a deceased loved one.

- ✦ Freedom: A bird dropping a white feather may be reminding you to think about what freedom means for you. Perhaps you're holding yourself back from true fulfilment.

In Roman mythology, the caladrius was a snow-white bird that dwelled in the king's palace and cured the inhabitants of illness. When it flew away, it dissolved any maladies, healing both itself and the patient.

Animal visitations

Have you ever noticed a robin arrive by your side and watch you right after a significant event, such as a loved one passing away? Or maybe you keep having dreams of an owl flying overhead, or an ant labouring away? Many traditions believe that animal visits or sightings are symbolic messages from the universe.

In Indigenous American or shamanic tradition, "power animals" are believed to be animals that can guide, teach and protect us. They can offer reassurance or comfort during a major life change, letting us know we're on the right path.

Take notice of any animals that you seem to share a moment with, either in the flesh or during a dream or meditation. They can also appear to you through intuition or telepathy. Be open to surprise and pay as much attention to a mouse as you would a tiger – your guides may not be the animals you expect!

Why this animal?

You may be bemused if you dream of a woodlouse, but these creatures can symbolize abundance or rebirth due to their resourcefulness and ability to convert waste into fuel. It's a good idea to do some research to understand why a particular animal has connected with you. It's also worth thinking about what this means to you and any cultural context. For example, some people fear snakes, whereas other societies worship them. The more you familiarize yourself with the animal, the more receptive you'll be to its messages.

Contemplate the following:

✦ Thinking about the animal's qualities and behaviours, are there any that it would serve you to adopt or shed?

✦ Are their behaviours relevant to things in your life? For example, does the animal have strong family bonds?

✦ Is the animal shining a light on habits you need to change? For example, perhaps it buries its head in the sand.

Common animal meanings

✦ **Owl:** Wisdom. The Roman goddess of wisdom, Minerva (Athena in Greek mythology) is often pictured with an owl.

✦ **Fox:** This cunning animal suggests the solution to a problem is at hand.

✦ **Ant:** Community and collaboration. The ant tells us that hard work lays the foundations for success.

✦ **Lion:** Strength, assertiveness and personal power.

✦ **Robin:** Renewal and transformation, as well as spiritual connection to loved ones who have passed over.

✦ **Tiger:** Vitality, physical and emotional strength, and patience.

✦ **Pig:** Good fortune, prosperity, fertility and self-acceptance.

✦ **Spider:** Communication and coordination, creativity, patience, feminine energy and receptivity, and being the weaver of your own destiny. They also represent the secretive aspects of your personality.

✦ **Snake:** Because they shed their skin, they're known to symbolize rebirth and transformation, healing, opportunity, temptation and sexuality (see also the ouroboros symbol, page 92).

You can use the journal pages of this book to explore what specific animals may mean to you.

Sacred geometry

The universe is said to be made up of geometric shapes that hold the blueprint for all life and creation. These shapes exist everywhere, from the perfect cell shapes of a tiny flower to sub-atomic particles that create planets. They are the building blocks of all life forms and without them there would be no universe!

Let's take a look at three of the most common sacred shapes and what message the universe may be trying to give you if you can't stop seeing them:

✦ The **circle** represents infinity, unity, oneness, wholeness, and the origin of everything, e.g. God, the divine, or whatever you believe the source of creation to be.

✦ The **triangle** is the dynamic force of creation and symbolizes fire, balance, harmony and the holy trinity.

✦ The **square** represents the stability of matter in the manifested physical world.

Circle

Associated with: Infinity, wholeness, oneness, unity, completion, renewal, protection, flow, commitment and focus, and the life cycle.

Numerical vibration: 1

Believed to be the oldest symbol used by humans, a circle has no beginning or end and is often associated with the wedding ring, representing eternal commitment. It has been used by all cultures across time and can be drawn with one single line. The celestial bodies in our galaxy, the planets, sun and moon are all spherical and appear circular at a distance. Our ancient ancestors used the circle as a protective boundary.

The circle is still used for protection worldwide, with stone circles prominent at sacred sites across the globe. Ancient circular symbols that we still value today include yin and yang, the chakras, ouroboros, tree of life and mandalas or medicine wheels used by Indigenous American people for health and healing.

Triangle

Associated with: Harmony, balance, unity, intuition, divine connection and psychic abilities, creation and creativity, inspiration, protection, fire, and raising and releasing energy.

Numerical vibration: 3

A triangle has three lines and three points. The number three represents the trinity, which can mean a number of things, such as mind, body and spirit, the Holy Trinity, or past, present and future.

Triangles direct energy and power towards the direction in which they point:

A triangle pointing up symbolizes a flame illuminating the darkness. Fire is seen as masculine, raising energy upwards to connect with the divine.

A triangle pointing downwards represents a cup that holds either water or spirit. This symbolizes feminine energy, receiving spiritual wisdom or anchoring energy into the earth.

Pointing to the right, a triangle symbolizes progression in life.

Pointing to the left, it suggests that you may be dwelling in the past.

Triangles have appeared in various cultures and spiritual practices since ancient times, with the number three considered the most sacred number.

North, South and Central America

Indigenous Americans are famous for their tepees – symbolizing "home".

Buddhism

The triangle is the symbol for enlightenment and access to higher knowledge.

Christianity

In Christianity, the triangle represents the Holy Trinity, meaning God as the Father, the Son (Jesus) and the Holy Spirit (or Holy Ghost).

The Eye of Providence

Related to the Trinity, the Eye of Providence is an all-seeing eye inside a triangle. It is still used by churches, institutions and some countries to symbolize an omnipresent and divine god watching over.

Ancient Egypt

The most famous triangles in the world are embodied in the Pyramids, which are made up of triangular faces. One of the most phenomenal constructions on earth, a pyramid in ancient Egypt represented life after death and directing energies towards the afterlife and the sun god Ra, creator of the world.

Star of David / Seal of Solomon

Mostly recognized as a Jewish symbol linked to King David, this star is also present in Islam as the Seal of Solomon, and in other cultures such as India. Two interlinking triangles, one pointing up and the other down, symbolize protection and the union of opposites in perfect harmony. The three-dimensional version of the Star of David is known as the merkaba, a vehicle of protective light that can transport your mind, body and spirit to higher dimensions.

Hinduism

The three points of the triangle represent the divine trinity: creation (Brahma), preservation (Vishnu) and destruction (Shiva). All chakra symbols also use equilateral triangles.

The sacred geometry symbol, Sri Yantra, is made of nine overlapping triangles that create 43 smaller triangles. This pattern is said to be the visual expression of the sound Om, considered to be the sound of creation. If you meditate on this symbol, it's believed to inspire enlightenment.

Square

Associated with: Stability, strength, endurance, strong foundations, boundaries, the four directions, seasons and elements, matter and the physical world, material manifestation, grounding, logic, law and order, and practicality and hard work.

Numerical vibration: 4

The square represents the physical laws of nature that provide us with a sense of security. It has the same significance across many religions and cultures and is believed to provide calm and security during times of stress or change. In a spiritual context, it often symbolizes integrity and can be seen as fixed or static. In Buddhism, the square symbolizes the foundation of a strong mind as well as the four noble truths (*dukkah* – suffering, *samudaya* – the cause of suffering, *nirodha* – the cessation of suffering, and *magga* – the path to liberation from suffering). This shape is also used in box breathing meditation.

In feng shui, the square can help relationships and family life to blossom. It's strongly associated with the element of Earth as it relates to laying foundations and establishing strong roots.

Genius is the ability to receive from the universe.

I Ching

Cosmic symbols from around the world

OUROBOROS

This popular symbol of the snake eating its tail reflects the cycle of birth, death and reincarnation. All these states of being must exist for the universe to stay in cosmic harmony and balance.

TREE OF LIFE

A symbol of cosmic connectivity that spans many cultures and religions, the tree of life shows our physical connection with the earth, while the branches reach towards the universe and spiritual enlightenment.

SHANKH OR CONCH SHELL

Particularly important to the Hindu religion, the shell is blown before rituals and ceremonies to connect with the spiritual world. It represents spiritual space and the bridge between the physical and divine realms. It resonates with the sound of Om, the creation frequency of the universe.

CROSS

Although mostly associated with Christianity, this symbol transcends religions. The vertical line is masculine, representing power and transcendence, while the horizontal line is feminine, grounded and wise. The two worlds meet at the axis, in a place of cosmic enlightenment connecting the spiritual and physical. The cross shape is reminiscent of the human body and the centre axis lies at the heart.

NORTH STAR

Some might say this is the ultimate symbol of the cosmos. The North Star shines down on Earth, illuminating the way and inspiring us to widen our knowledge of the world through travel and discovery. It's a constant in our lives and can guide us forwards and be a beacon of hope. It reminds us to trust in something greater than ourselves – the universe – and that we are never truly lost; we can always find our way back.

Chapter Four

DREAMS

For as long as humankind has existed, so have dreams. In ancient times, people revered dreams and visions so highly that they actively sought them out.

Dream interpretations have been found on clay tablets in Mesopotamia (modern-day Iraq) dating as far back as 3000–4000 BCE, which means we've been trying to figure out our dreams for at least 6,000 years.

Dreams are another way in which the universe sends us signals, whether it's through a divine or spiritual messenger or via our subconscious minds. This chapter explores the history of dreams as divine visions, the role of the subconscious and some tips on how to remember and interpret your dreams. There's also a short section on common dream motifs to get you started.

A dream which
is not interpreted
is like a letter that
is not read.

The Babylonian Talmud,
an ancient Jewish text

Dreams as signs from the universe

Dreams have been considered as messages from the universe since ancient times, from early humans who viewed dreams as an indication of their god's will (or the haunting of the Devil), through to today's interest in searching our dreams for significant life guidance.

Some people claim to predict the future in dreams. You can practise this skill simply by noting down your dreams and looking for patterns or coincidences that then emerge in your waking life. Prophecy is considered a major sign of synchronicity from the universe! It's important to remember that dream interpretation varies between cultures and individuals, as well as across time.

Types of dream

According to the US National Sleep Foundation, we can have anything between four and six dreams per night, making for a total of around 2 hours of (hopefully) sweet dreams. We're most likely to dream in the REM phase of sleep (where the eyes dart quickly under the lids and the brain is as active as while we're awake), with a new REM cycle starting every 90 minutes.

Dreams can take many forms:

✦ **Nightmares:** These are the unpleasant, fear-based dreams with distressing content that we've all experienced.

✦ **Vivid dreams:** Super realistic dreams with very clear images and messages.

✦ **Psychic and precognitive dreams or visions:** These can predict the future or show us something revelatory.

✦ **Recurring dreams:** These continually nag at you with the same repeating imagery or theme.

✦ **Lucid dreams:** These occur when a person is aware they're dreaming and can consciously control the dream they're in.

Dreams as visions

A vision is something startling and powerful, deemed to be of supernatural origin and can be seen in a dream or even during full consciousness. One of the most famous visions occurred in Christianity when Mary is said to have seen the Angel Gabriel, who told her she'd give birth to a son, Jesus.

Visions are said to convey revelatory and life-changing messages and are sometimes experienced more clearly during consciousness than when they appear in dreams. Prophecy is associated with visions and they are linked throughout history to spiritual tradition and communication from the spiritual realm. Visions seen in dreams may be called "psychic" or "prophetic" dreams and are said to convey messages from the divine. Some people believe that if you're receptive to the universe's messages, dreams and visions can increase creativity.

The history of dreams as visions

While dreams have multiple functions, visions were, historically, mostly religious or spiritual in nature. Many ancient texts focus on "visitation dreams" which is where a god or ancestor would instruct the dreamer to do something or predict the future.

Ancient Egypt

The Ancient Egyptians believed their gods showed themselves in dreams and visions, and they categorized three types of dream: those in which the gods demanded something, warning dreams, and visions that came to them during dream rituals.

Some temples had "dream beds" where people could rest in the hope that they would receive a vision of guidance, comfort or healing. Citizens who had vivid and profound dreams were seen as a cut above the rest and dream interpreters were revered as divinely gifted individuals. Given their link to the divine, priests in ancient Egypt often performed these interpretation duties.

Ancient Greece

Citizens of Ancient Greece relied heavily on dreams or visions as a form of religious guidance, seeing them as warnings or prophecies. The Greeks adhered to a strict cleansing ritual before entering the temple. No sex, meat or fish was permitted for 48 hours and they could only drink water. An animal sacrifice would be made to the god they wished to connect with. They would then enter the temple and lie on the skin of the animal they'd sacrificed, hoping for insightful dreams.

Ancient Rome

The Roman statesman Cicero wrote that the deceased grandfather of consul Scipio Aemilianus taught his grandson the secrets of the cosmos in a dream. The fifth-century CE Roman writer Macrobius defined five types of dream in his *Commentarii in Somnium Scipionis*: symbolic dreams, revelatory visions, oracle dreams (the appearance of an ancestor, angel or deity giving wisdom), worthless daydreams and mind fritterings.

Visions in Judaism and Christianity

Visions play a huge role in both the Old and New Testaments, such as Jacob's vision of the ladder leading to Heaven. In Old English religious texts, the dreams and visions of saints encourage devotion and virtue, while sinners are tormented with reprimands from God. During the Middle Ages, dreams were interpreted as temptations from the Devil, who was said to corrupt people's minds when they were vulnerable, namely asleep.

Visions in art

Throughout history, dreams and visions have inspired famous creative works, such as Chaucer's *Parliament of Fowls* (*c.* 1382) and the anonymous late fourteenth-century poem *Pearl*, which uses the dream vision to reflect on the nature of grief and loss.

At the court of Charles VI of France, Christine de Pizan, fed up with the misogyny of court literature, wrote *The Book of the City of Ladies* (1405), featuring dream characters Reason, Rectitude and Justice.

Dreams and the subconscious

Modern dream interpretation, introduced by Sigmund Freud (1856–1939) and Carl Jung (1875–1961), suggests that dreams carry deep revelations from our subconscious.

When we sleep, our rational mind rests, allowing things in our subconscious mind to come to the surface. Our subconscious is part of our consciousness, but it's often not in full focus during our daily lives. We're likely to have thoughts and feelings that we may repress on a daily basis, as well as behavioural patterns that we're not aware of.

The subconscious tries to bring these areas for improvement to our attention and it does this when we're in our most relaxed state – while we're asleep. This is also when we're more receptive to universal energies and messages so the universe can utilize our subconscious as a tool for our own awakening.

How to improve dream recall through intention

We've all had the experience where we've woke up confused because we had the most bizarre or even awful dream. What did it all mean? Our job is then to play detective and piece it together – remember, the universe is trying to help rather than scare us. But often we're left with the vaguest sense of what we dreamed about, because of the ephemeral nature of dreams, and because we can't remember many of the details.

Here are some ideas to help you improve your memory of those all-important reveries:

✦ Research shows that if you make a conscious decision to remember your dreams before going to bed, you're more likely to succeed. So, make this a deliberate intention before you switch off the light.

✦ Keep a journal by your bed. Make it as easy as you can to piece together those clues.

✦ Research also shows we're more likely to remember dreams when we wake up in the middle of them. If you find yourself waking up during the night, jot down what you can remember. Think about the emotion of the dream and note down any images, sensations or words that may jog your memory when you read over your notes at a later date.

✦ As soon as you wake up in the morning, keep your eyes closed and replay the dreams in your mind. In this way, you're reviewing them as you enter your waking state. This should help you to remember them just like any other memory.

You could treat yourself to a fancy dream journal or there are smartphone apps that can help you create an organized and searchable digital journal. The more you practise dream recall, the better you'll get at it!

Dream recall with crystals

Not only are certain crystals excellent for improving sleep, they can also help you to recall your dreams. Some crystals carry energy that can help us with anything, from providing a deeper REM state to improving dream recall.

Follow the steps below to improve dream recall with a crystal:

1   Select your crystal.

2   Tuck yourself up comfortably in bed and then intentionally connect with your crystal by placing it on your third eye in the middle of your forehead. Or you can hold it in your left hand, which is said to be your "receiving" hand.

3   Focus on your intention for either your sleep or your dreams. For example, "I intend to recall my dreams in the morning" or "I intend to have a peaceful sleep" or "I would like to receive a message in my dream regarding X." Say your affirmation three times.

4   Place the crystal under your pillow or bed or on your bedside table.

5   Turn the light out and Zzzzzzz!

6   On waking, write down what you can remember from your dreams before you do anything else.

Trying one at a time, experiment to find out which crystals suit you best. You can choose from the selection below:

✦ **Amethyst:** Encourages peaceful rest and pleasant dreams.

✦ **Herkimer diamond (double-terminated clear quartz):** Cleanses your energy as you sleep and helps you to recall those hidden messages.

✦ **Lapis lazuli:** Encourages vivid dreams and provides deep insight into their meaning.

✦ **Fluorite:** Balances the mind and allows for more restful sleep and clearer dreams.

✦ **Celestite:** A high vibration stone that aids connection with the spiritual realm and eases anxiety to promote peaceful sleep.

✦ **Moonstone:** Protects against negative dream states with its connection to the moon and feminine energy.

✦ **Jade:** Attracts helpful spirit guides if you're requiring answers or solutions from your dreams.

The basics of dream interpretation

Our dreams always offer us guidance, whether that's in the form of visions, psychic or precognitive dreams, or through messages from our own subconscious. Dream dictionaries are a useful starting point, but journalling our dreams and becoming familiar with our own inner psychological landscape is the best approach. Ultimately there's no objective way to interpret dreams and you should listen closely to your gut feeling – you're the one who knows yourself best and what's happening in your life. Often, the universe is working through your subconscious to flag up something for resolution, although a small number of dreams may be prophetic.

Look for the following signs in order to grasp what last night's strange meanderings are trying to tell you:

Emotions

How did you feel during the dream and on waking up? This feeling is a great guide to what your dream means, as your current emotional state about something is being shown to you.

Themes

Are you fed up with having the same dream over and over again? The universe is really trying to get something through to you! If your dreams are repeating on you, try and work out what the common theme is, as that's what needs to be addressed.

Symbols

Dreams are full of symbols! Always consider each symbol's personal or cultural meaning to you. For example, dreaming of fish will have a different meaning for a devout Christian than it will for a fisher!

Who is in your dream?

Dreams act like mirrors – whoever we see in our dream will be reflecting our behaviour back at us. What does the person in the dream symbolize to you? Might they be showing you ways in which you'd like to behave, or the opposite?

Common dream imagery

Our dreams are often loaded with symbolism. All we need to do is decode these hidden messages from the universe and our subconscious. Here are some common dream motifs and their meanings:

Actor: Seeing your favourite actor and the role they're playing for you in your dream could be reflecting some element of behaviour or personality back to you. Perhaps they're showing you what you'd like to be?

Climbing: Often a metaphor for overcoming obstacles or gaining a new understanding about something.

Falling: An anxiety dream signifying that you feel insecure or powerless in some aspect of your life.

Fish: An ancient Christian symbol regarded as a sign of spirituality, fortune and nourishment. Alternatively, check whether there's something "fishy" about a situation, or perhaps you're feeling like a fish out of water.

Flying: Do you feel in control during your waking life? If so, your flying will feel effortless. If you're struggling to fly in dreams, there may be difficulties to overcome in your real life. Perhaps you're in a phase of transition or growth.

Naked: A potential indicator that you feel vulnerable and exposed in some situation. Or, alternatively, it can mean you're comfortable in your own skin.

Parcel: Perhaps a sign you're about to receive something exciting in your life!

Phone: Do you need to talk to someone, or perhaps there's a particular message you need to hear? If the phone rings in the dream and you don't answer, this could mean you're ignoring something.

Snakes: These creatures can highlight a negative emotion such as fear or a hidden threat. Or they can hint at something positive, such as change and renewal. They can also have sexual connotations.

Teeth: Are you feeling anxious or powerless about something? Dreams about teeth falling out can also mean you're worried about your appearance.

Water: The symbol of your unconscious that reflects your emotions. The state of the water (calm, choppy, muddy etc.) represents your emotional state in waking life.

Chapter Five

GUT FEELINGS and INTUITION

Studies have estimated that a trillion bits of information enter our senses every second, but only a fraction of that ever makes it into consciousness. Yet our unconscious mind picks up all kinds of signals that we're not aware of.

This chapter looks at gut feelings and intuition, exploring what this means, what it feels like to receive a gut feeling from the universe and how we can tune into those all important signals that our unconscious mind is picking up. There's a wealth of guidance on offer to us every second of the day that could be showing us anything, such as the right job to go for or even ways to save our own lives.

Gut feeling, "hunch" or intuition

Have you ever been told to trust your gut? Sometimes we just know something's up without being able to put a finger on why.

The word intuition comes either from the Latin verb *intueri* ("consider") or from the late-Middle English word intuit, "to contemplate". It's a term that's been used for centuries in philosophy, psychology and spirituality to refer to the ability to understand without conscious reasoning or factual evidence. Some people call this psychic ability, but it's available to us all! It's described by many as a higher level of consciousness – the capacity to sense energies and make good choices based on your reading of those energies. It's about thriving, rather than just surviving.

Intuition is a subconscious process that comes from beyond the five senses, which earns it the name "the sixth sense". It brings information and solutions into the conscious mind through the third eye chakra. This information then moves down to the gut, translating to a physical feeling that alerts us to something either being very right or very wrong.

Where does intuition come from?

✦ Knowledge stored in the subconscious mind.

✦ Telepathy or psychic connection to higher realms, accessing knowledge not available to the five senses.

✦ Subconscious interpretation of body language.

✦ Very quick understanding of a problem or situation that's too quick for the reasoning mind.

✦ Accessing the collective unconscious, namely concepts and biases shared by all human beings that we may not be aware of.

Gut instinct

We may also experience a "gut instinct" to flee a certain person, situation or event. This instinct is slightly different from a gut feeling or intuition as it's a tendency that is hardwired in us for survival and reproduction. You could say this is a sign from the universe working through the biology that it so cleverly designed.

Science vs spiritual

The science bit

Scientists agree that what we feel in the body is the result of complex processes that happen in the brain. Every day, your brain processes sensory data from your environment. Some of this information you're aware of, for example, if you notice an argument between two people, you'll probably cross the street to avoid it. This is a rational decision based on the information available.

Your brain carries out these automatic processes because it wants to predict what might happen next and keep you safe. It bases these predictions on previous knowledge and experiences. These brain processes run in the background, a bit like computer software programs. When the brain makes a good match or mismatch between what's in front of us and our "software programs", it sends signals to the gut, which is full of nerve cells. It's no wonder that we then get butterflies in the stomach, nausea or other twinges, leading to a "gut feeling".

The spiritual view

Catharine Allan, a clairvoyant, intuitive and author of *A Little Bit of Intuition*, says "people usually get an overall sensation of knowing" if something's off. How that knowing presents itself manifests differently for everyone. As intuition guides our gut feelings, each of us might experience them in different ways, depending on which of the following four "clairs" we are most sensitive to:

Clairvoyance: Clear sight or being able to see into the future.
 Gut feeling would manifest a visual image.

Claircognizance: Clear knowing.
 Gut feeling would present as thoughts.

Clairsentience: Clear feeling, sensing information through the body.
 Gut feeling would be a physical sensation.

Clairaudience: Clear hearing.
Gut feeling would present as words dropping into your head.

Which of the four clairs are you?

Some lucky readers who are extra sensitive may have all four, but most of us will have one or two that are more dominant. Take the quiz below to see which "clair" you are.

How do you like to learn new information?

a) Visual information such as videos.

b) Information given verbally, either directly or by audio.

c) Through personal experience – by doing or feeling.

d) You enjoy learning from research; you love facts and developing your knowledge.

You fancy a holiday. How do you choose?

a) From those beautiful pictures of palm trees! You get excited when you see them and your energy rises.

b) An inner voice says to you, "This is the place!"

c) Based on a previous trip that you thoroughly enjoyed.

d) An inner instinct tells you which trip to pick. You just know!

You're at a party and your intuition is telling you it's time to leave. How do you receive the message?

a) You picture yourself sitting at home, comfy on the sofa while reading a book.

b) You hear a voice say, "It's OK if you need to go."

c) You feel tired and your energy has suddenly become low.

d) You realize it's the perfect time to leave as you can catch the last train.

Your intuition is telling you a job interview is going to go well. How does it communicate this to you?

a) You see a happy image of yourself and picture how you will feel in the job.

b) You hear a calm, reassuring voice saying, "This is the job for you."

c) You get good vibes from the office when you arrive for your interview and feel you'd fit in.

d) You suddenly get some "downloads" in your head of some great examples you want to share in the interview.

How did you score?

Mostly a: You are clairvoyant

Mostly b: You are clairaudient

Mostly c: You are clairsentient

Mostly d: You are claircognizant

Clairvoyant

Clairvoyants receive messages as images they see in their mind's eye, which are usually symbolic or metaphorical.

Developing your skill: Note down or sketch any images you receive, including dreams and premonitions. Divinatory tools like tarot cards may give further clarity. Regular meditation allows time and space for your visions to flourish.

Clairaudient

If you're clairaudient, you'll hear calm and clear messages that sound like a voice talking in your mind.

Developing your skill: Becoming a better listener is the key to making the most of this skill. Go somewhere quiet and really tune into the sounds around you, to see what you pick up. Exposure to many different sounds (such as a wide variety of music) can help you to notice subtle differences.

Clairsentient

The most common of the clairs, those who are clairsentient receive intuition through physical, emotional or energetic feelings. Clairsentients may be overrun with gut feelings.

Developing your skill: Journalling to record your feelings is super useful for a clairsentient. It'll help you to make sense of your body's reactions and any other patterns in your feelings. It's important to assert your boundaries and protect your personal space since you're so sensitive to the energies of others. Strengthen your connection with your body through yoga and massage.

Claircognizant

Intuitive thoughts drop into your head, like downloads from somewhere! You may feel instant insight or "knowing" about something or someone.

Developing your skill: Stream of consciousness writing (see page 132) is a great tool for you. You'll need to record your downloads quickly before they disappear. Communicating your thoughts with others can also be a good way to solidify your intuition.

Blocks to intuition

In the modern world, physical and factual evidence is often relied on. Many of us are taught that it's not possible to receive information from spiritual sources, and sceptics may question how we can "just know" something. We will often be doubted or told that the information we receive isn't accurate which can cause us to lose faith in our intuition and psychic abilities.

Fear is the biggest barrier to receiving information from your third eye and your gut as it will block the flow, reducing the messages and sensations that come freely when your mind is open and trusting. Keeping your auras clean, your awareness high and allowing your intuition to make sense of universal energy and your subconscious can help you resolve this.

We can choose to open our minds, to believe, receive and feel. Having the courage to do this could make a real difference in our lives.

How to develop your intuition

Intuitive and medium Jill Willard suggests:

1   Taking quiet time to experience stillness.

2   Taking time to stretch your body.

3   Meditating with your third eye or brow chakra (see page 126).

4   Walking in nature, swimming in the wild or practising yoga.

5   Focusing on being present and making "being" as important as "doing". It's when we're in a state of "being" that we'll be more in tune with our intuition.

6   Making more eye contact with those we love and focusing on our connections with others.

7   Making sure your chakras are balanced. If your chakras are out of balance, this can block your ability to heal and hinder your naturally intuitive nature (see page 32 on how to cleanse your aura and chakras).

What is the third eye?

The third eye chakra is the sixth energy centre in the body's seven chakra system, and it is located between the eyebrows. This chakra is our inner guidance system and our best tool for self-reflection. It gives us access to universal wisdom and truths, and is associated with the colour indigo.

The third eye governs the mind, psychic connection, intuition, wisdom, intellect, inspiration, imagination, awakening, clairvoyance, clarity of thought and decision-making.

Signs of a balanced third eye chakra: Freedom of thought and expression, detachment from illusions, psychic ability, increased ability for self-reflection and meditation, releasing limiting beliefs and fears, realization that change is inevitable and that death is not the end, and that mistakes are lessons to learn from.

Signs of an unbalanced third eye chakra: Behaviour driven by fears and limiting beliefs, inability to see the bigger picture, mind closed to spiritual and psychic connection, unable to separate truth and illusion, indecisiveness, lack of clarity and purpose, unwillingness to accept the truth about ourselves, fear of criticism and feeling stuck.

Physical symptoms of a blocked third eye chakra:

✦ Headaches

✦ Depression

✦ Clumsiness

✦ Sleep disorders and nightmares

✦ Eye and sinus issues, hormone imbalances
  and burnout

With this chakra fully opened, you'll find your psychic abilities and intuition flourishing like never before and discover a new sense of clarity and purpose enabling you to take confident strides towards your goals. Your view of the world and the universe will open right up, you'll be able to see everything from a wider perspective and find a balance between emotion and reason.

Opening your third eye with crystals

The following crystals are excellent for opening your third eye and working with intuition:

Lapis lazuli, larimar, amethyst, labradorite, sodalite, azurite, moonstone, celestite, kyanite, lepidolite.

Try the following meditation to open your third eye with the power of crystals:

1   Place your chosen crystal in the middle of your forehead, slightly above your brow.

2   Sit comfortably as you normally would for meditation, close your eyes and focus on your breath.

3   Breathe in deeply through your nose and exhale slowly through your mouth.

4   As you breathe, visualize an indigo-coloured light emanating from the crystal in the middle of your forehead. Breathe into the light and imagine it expanding and becoming brighter. Continue to breathe deeply, focusing on the light and visualizing it opening your third eye chakra.

5   Imagine it expanding until your whole field of vision is filled with light. Hold the visualization for as long as you like, then slowly release it.

Use these affirmations during meditation, or at any time, to strengthen your connection with your third eye:

✦   I am wise and connected to my inner voice.

✦   I trust myself and my higher power.

How long does it take to open your third eye?

For some, it happens straight away or over a few days, although it can take much longer. It could take years or even a lifetime of practice to cultivate.

How do you know when your third eye is open?

Once you send out the signal to the universe that you'd like to begin working with your third eye, you'll start to receive guidance, such as messages and visions. The more you're able to connect, understand and work with your intuition, the more your third eye strength will grow.

What do "gut feelings" feel like?

We discovered earlier that intuition translates into physical feelings in the body – both positive and negative. The negative responses are linked to anxiety and can serve as a warning.

Here are some signs of a gut feeling:

✦ Tension in your body

✦ A flash of clarity

✦ Goosebumps or prickling sensation

✦ Butterflies in your stomach

✦ Increased heart rate

✦ A sinking feeling in the pit of your stomach

✦ Sweaty palms or feet

✦ Recurring thoughts that won't go away relating to a specific person or situation

✦ A feeling of peace once a decision has been made and you feel absolutely certain it was the right one.

Some of these feelings might come on so strongly that you can't ignore them. At other times, you might just feel a faint sense of uneasiness. It's good practice to pay attention to the signals your unconscious mind is sending your body, no matter how slight.

What are gut feelings trying to tell you?

Your gut feelings can be trying to tell you all sorts of things. Here are some of the most common messages from your gut:

1 **You're in danger:** The most primal and evolutionary response to keep us safe.

2 **Something feels physically wrong in your body:** We know our bodies better than anyone else, so we can often detect any changes and imbalances. If your gut is telling you something's abnormal, get it checked out.

3 **This person or situation is good:** Maybe a person you've just met gives you a good vibe. You may get a warm, safe or happy feeling in your tummy.

4 **This person or situation is not good:** You may feel anxiety, tension or even disgust or nausea in the gut.

5 **Take the risk:** You're feeling like moving somewhere completely different. Where did that come from? Sometimes our intuition knows what's right for us before our conscious mind does, but we may try to override it with logic as that's what we've been taught. But if you ignore your gut, it can lead to problems further down the road, so do so at your peril!

How to trust your gut

Tuning in to your emotions and any physical sensations in your body can help you practise listening to your gut and learning when to trust it. But here are some other points to consider:

1   Are your instincts or feelings being clouded by unconscious biases and prejudices, such as anxieties from a previous experience, or a "good" feeling because the sun is shining? When making an important decision, take a step back and see if you can identify any conscious or unconscious biases.

2   Do you need to make a decision immediately (for example, if you're driving), or do you have time to back up your gut feeling with logic or hard evidence (for instance, when deciding whether to accept a job)? Taking time to decide objectively can help avoid knee-jerk reactions.

3   Consider any contrary evidence that may go against your gut. Is this compelling enough to give you second thoughts?

Journalling

Did you ever keep a diary as a child but grow out of it when you reached adulthood because of the increasing demands of life?

It's easy to underestimate the importance of journalling, but by writing down your thoughts and feelings, you'll gain a great insight into the patterns running through your life. It's one of the best tools to use for understanding yourself better. It can help you to express yourself when you feel unable to do so and it can be extremely useful to help process feelings.

You can be as creative as you wish, making your journal a fun place to hang out. You can use coloured pens and illustrations or include quotes that inspire you. And guess what – the more insight you gain into your thoughts and feelings, the more in tune you'll be with your intuition!

Stream of consciousness writing and Morning Pages

Stream of consciousness writing involves writing everything that comes into your head without stopping.

The writer Julia Cameron recommends this practice in her book *The Artist's Way* as a way to clear out any unwanted clutter in your mind. By clearing our mental and emotional detritus, our aura becomes clearer and the link to our unconscious mind strengthens. And sometimes this means, when you re-read your writing afterwards, you may discover some truths about your life staring you in the face. Cameron calls this practice Morning Pages.

Follow the steps below to write Morning Pages:

1   The clue's in the name – Morning Pages are, according to Cameron, best done in the morning. Complete them in bed first thing or early on before you go about your day.

2   Always write by hand with a pen/pencil and paper. Cameron believes this allows us to have a deeper connection with ourselves than if we're typing. For one thing, it would certainly interrupt spontaneous flow if you were having to continuously correct predictive text!

3   Write three pages without stopping. Keep the pen moving, and if your stream of consciousness flow dries up, write "I am writing" until your brain moves on to something else and gets going again.

4   Don't worry about what you're writing – you don't even need to think about it. It doesn't matter if it's not even full sentences! Then, read your pages over for any flashes of insight or creative ideas, or simply rip them up when you're done. Unlike journalling, you don't have to keep them, and it's important for this to be for your eyes only so that you can feel free to truly be yourself.

Intuition and divinatory tools

Divinatory tools are fortune-telling methods like tarot, oracle and angel cards, runes, *I Ching* and even water divination. When we use these methods, we're usually looking for answers and seeking connection with a higher universal power to give us guidance. A good card reader or diviner will always use the intuition that comes to them to enhance their reading.

Always use the booklets that come with fortune-telling cards, then allow your intuition to come in. Along with receiving insights into what the future holds, with practice you'll get to know yourself and your desires. The more self-awareness you develop, the better equipped you'll be to interpret the signs from the universe.

If your reading doesn't come up with the answers you were hoping for, don't worry. It may be that it's not the right time or there is no answer to your question yet – but trust in the process and know that the universe is always looking out for you.

The importance of self-awareness

Self-awareness is vital when it comes to divination, gut feelings and intuition. The more you know yourself, the easier it will be to interpret the signals and synchronicities you're receiving, and the stronger your inner guidance system will be. Always remember that your inner guidance system is inextricably linked to the guidance system of the universe, because you are a part of it!

Many people go through life without much self-awareness, but making active choices to develop healthy patterns of behaviour will increase your ability to stay in touch with your intuition and cosmic signs. Life can be unpredictable, but being aware of your reactions, patterns, strengths and weaknesses can help you keep a clear head when you need it most, helping your intuition to guide you through.

Déjà vu

All of us will have experienced the odd feeling that is déjà vu. But what exactly is it and what is the universe trying to tell us? Meaning "already seen" in French, déjà vu is a feeling of familiarity that you can't quite put your finger on. You think you may have experienced this moment before but don't know when or where. This isn't the universe trying to creep us out – it's trying to help us out!

Déjà vu can be a symbol of spiritual communication or heightened intuition, and it may be telling you the following:

1   You've experienced this moment, situation or place in a past life.

2   Your ancestral memories are being triggered. It's believed by some that we carry the energetic imprints of our ancestors from at least seven generations back.

3   You may have foreseen this moment in a dream.

4   Your vibrational frequency exactly matches a person or place, triggering feelings of déjà vu.

Intuition is
the whisper
of the soul.

Jiddu Krishnamurti

Farewell

In this book, we've explored paying attention to the universe's signals, the meaning of synchronicity and meaningful coincidences, and all different kinds of signs from the universe. We've discussed concepts such as vibrations, manifestation and universal energy and the role they play in how the cosmos communicates with us. We've also considered signs that arrive to us through dreams, angels and spirit guides, and common symbols from the universe and its messengers, such as numbers, coins, flowers and even traditional shapes.

This journey should leave you with a better understanding of what you're looking for next time you're seeking divine guidance. By continuing to follow the advice in this book, you can hone your manifestation skills and feel reassured that you're moving in the right direction. Working with the universe instead of against it can be truly life-changing. Once you begin to pick up on the signs, you won't be able to stop!

Signs from the universe can offer enormous comfort and make us feel connected to all that surrounds us. They reassure us that there's something out there looking after us, no matter what. All we have to do is see it.

JOURNAL PAGES

Journalling or writing down the signs you receive will help you to decipher the language of the universe. This is so that you can note synchronicities and build an understanding of what each sign means to you – especially if the meaning is not immediately clear to you without further consideration.

The following pages feature some handy prompts based on the chapters in this book. Feel free to scribble away, noting details of any signs you've been sent from the universe in whatever form (whether through dreams, angel or spirit guides, animals, ancestors, etc.). As you continue to journal, you'll become better at understanding your own inner guidance system and might not be able to write the signs down quick enough.

Don't forget to add any later developments as your awareness and sensitivity to universal energy continues to grow.

Chapter One
What are signs from the universe?

Date: ....

How have you connected to universal energy today?

....

....

How did it affect you?

....

....

What are your short-term desires or goals?

....

....

What steps can you take to manifest them?

....

....

Date: . . . .

How have you connected to universal energy today?

. . . .

. . . .

. . . .

How did it affect you?

. . . .

. . . .

. . . .

What are your short-term desires or goals?

. . . .

. . . .

. . . .

What steps can you take to manifest them?

. . . .

. . . .

. . . .

Chapter Two
Angels and spirit guides

Date . . . .

Tick off the following angel signs that you've seen this week:

☐ White feather   ☐ Dreams

☐ Rainbow   ☐ Books

☐ Angel numbers   ☐ Advert

Other angel signs that you've seen (for example, this could include coins or shapes in clouds, as per the symbols chapter):

. . . .

. . . .

Any particular scents or sounds that you've noticed:

. . . .

. . . .

What do the signs you've experienced mean to you, and how might they relate to your current life situation?

. . . .

. . . .

Date: . . . .

Recurring number sequences you have seen recently:

. . . .

. . . .

What do these numbers mean according to the guide in this book?

. . . .

. . . .

. . . .

What images or thoughts did you get when you saw this number?

. . . .

. . . .

. . . .

What does this number mean to you?

. . . .

. . . .

. . . .

Chapter Three
Symbols

Date: ....

What recurring symbol do you keep noticing?

....

....

What were you thinking about at the time you saw the symbol?

....

....

Have you looked up traditional meanings of the symbol? Which meanings might apply to your current situation?

....

....

Do you have any of your own thoughts, feelings or intuitions about what the symbol might represent for you?

....

....

Date: . . . .

What recurring symbol do you keep noticing?

. . . .

. . . .

. . . .

What were you thinking about at the time you saw the symbol?

. . . .

. . . .

. . . .

Have you looked up traditional meanings of the symbol?
Which meanings might apply to your current situation?

. . . .

. . . .

. . . .

Do you have any of your own thoughts, feelings or intuitions
about what the symbol might represent for you?

. . . .

. . . .

. . . .

Chapter Four
Dreams

Date: . . . .

Type of dream: . . . .

Description of my dream:

. . . .

Emotions that I felt on waking:

. . . .

Symbols that appeared in my dream:

. . . .

How the dream relates to how I feel inside, or a current
situation in my life:

. . . .

What the universe could be trying to tell me about this:

. . . .

Return at a later date and add any developments that shed
new meaning on the dream:

. . . .

Date: . . . .

Type of dream: . . . .

Description of my dream:

. . . .

. . . .

Emotions that I felt on waking:

. . . .

. . . .

Symbols that appeared in my dream:

. . . .

How the dream relates to how I feel inside, or a current
situation in my life:

. . . .

What the universe could be trying to tell me about this:

. . . .

Return at a later date and add any developments that shed
new meaning on the dream:

. . . .

. . . .

Date: . . . .

Type of dream: . . . .

Description of my dream:

. . . .

. . . .

Emotions that I felt on waking:

. . . .

. . . .

Symbols that appeared in my dream:

. . . .

How the dream relates to how I feel inside, or a current situation in my life:

. . . .

What the universe could be trying to tell me about this:

. . . .

Return at a later date and add any developments that shed new meaning on the dream:

. . . .

. . . .

Date: . . . .

Type of dream: . . . .

Description of my dream:

. . . .

. . . .

Emotions that I felt on waking:

. . . .

. . . .

Symbols that appeared in my dream:

. . . .

How the dream relates to how I feel inside, or a current
situation in my life:

. . . .

What the universe could be trying to tell me about this:

. . . .

Return at a later date and add any developments that shed
new meaning on the dream:

. . . .

. . . .

Chapter Five
Gut feelings and intuition

Date: . . . .

Can you think of a time recently when you experienced a gut feeling or intuition?

. . . .

. . . .

Did you experience any physical sensations in your body? If so, what were they?

. . . .

. . . .

Did you get a "knowing" sensation, or any other feelings or thoughts?

. . . .

. . . .

Did you act on your gut feeling or intuition? If so, in what way?

. . . .

. . . .

Did your gut feeling or intuition turn out to be right?

. . . .

. . . .

. . . .

If not, what factors could have interfered? Are there any biases you weren't aware of at the time?

. . . .

. . . .

. . . .

If your intuition was right, how did this change your path?

. . . .

. . . .

. . . .

Have you worked with opening your third eye? If so, what were your experiences (e.g. images, sensations, etc.)?

. . . .

. . . .

. . . .

Morning Pages

Use the next three pages of this journal to write your first
Morning Pages (as described on page 132 of this book).

Remember to write these by hand, and to keep that pen
flowing without stopping.

Use the fourth page to gain insight into what you've
written.

....

....

....

....

....

....

....

....

....

....

....

....

....

How did writing the Morning Pages make you feel?

. . . .

. . . .

Was there anything you discovered about yourself?

. . . .

. . . .

Did you receive any clarity about a situation?

. . . .

. . . .

Did you uncover any hidden wisdom or nuggets of truth from your inner self or the universe?

. . . .

. . . .

Have the pages inspired any creative ideas?

. . . .

. . . .

Will you be doing Morning Pages again? (You can even buy yourself a nice journal, especially for the job!)

. . . .

. . . .

Hocus Focus

Corinne Marley

ISBN: 978-1-83799-188-4

Conjure the magic within you with this modern guide to the ancient art of spell-work and manifestation – all you need is a little hocus focus

Including a variety of spells for every place and occasion – and tips and tricks on how to cast them – this enchanting book is the perfect introduction to invoking the universal energies at your disposal. Complete with fill-in sections to chronicle your experiences, this collection of rituals will guide you to a path of infinite possibilities, help you develop your unique gifts and abilities, and set you well on your way to creating the life you have always wanted.

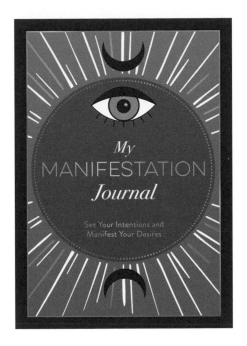

My Manifestation Journal

Astrid Carvel

ISBN: 978-1-80007-829-1

Turn your dreams into reality with the help of this guided manifestation journal

What if everything your heart desired was just a flick of a pen away? Whether you dream of securing the perfect job, having better health or finding love, writing down your manifestations may be the key to turning your aspirations into reality. Whether you're a beginner or a more seasoned manifester, these beautiful journal pages provide everything you need to create the life of your dreams.

Have you enjoyed this book? If so, find us
on Facebook at **Summersdale Publishers,** on
Twitter at **@Summersdale** and on Instagram and
TikTok at **@summersdalebooks** and get in touch.
We'd love to hear from you!

www.summersdale.com

Image Credits